PENGUINS, FALCONS,

FINCHES AND OTHER BIRDS

Alex Edmonds

Franklin Watts

LONDON ● SYDNEY

© Aladdin Books Ltd 1998
Designed and produced by
Aladdin Books Ltd
28 Percy Street
London W1P 0LD

*First published in Great Britain
in 1998 by*
Franklin Watts
96 Leonard Street
London EC2A 4RH

A catalogue record for this book is available from the
British Library.

ISBN: 0 7496 2830 8

Editor
Michael Flaherty

Designer
Jeff Gurney

Picture Research
Brooks Krikler Research

Front cover illustration
Gary Edgar-Hyde

Illustrators include
Rob Shone
John Rignall
Adrian Lascom, Garden Studios
Creative Hands

Certain illustrations have appeared in
earlier books created by Aladdin Books.

The consultant, Joyce Pope, did her first degree in
geography. She has worked for many years as a
lecturer at the Natural History Museum. She now
studies, writes and lectures about animals.

Printed in Belgium

CONTENTS

INTRODUCTION

Birds have managed to conquer every part of the world. They are the most abundant of all warm-blooded animals. They exist alongside humans and take advantage of things like freshly grown crops for food. They may also suffer in places where humans use pesticides or destroy their habitats. The success of birds depends on their ability to fly. This has allowed them to make use of habitats and food sources that other animals cannot reach. Whether pet or pest, birds bring the air alive with their song and flight.

The skeleton

Birds are vertebrates. This means that they have a backbone, and they have a bony skeleton. The skeleton of birds that can fly is very light. This helps to reduce the effort needed to fly. The weight is kept to a minimum by having hollow bones. The inside of the bones of a flying bird is like honeycomb. This structure gives them strength. The breastbone of flying birds also has a large keel. This provides a place to anchor the huge pectoral (chest) muscles needed to power their flight.

The first birds appeared over 150 million years ago. Today, birds are found in all shapes and sizes, but there are some features they all have in common. They are covered in feathers. They all have beaks for feeding. They are warm-blooded, like mammals. They lay eggs, like many reptiles. They have wings, as do bats, though some birds cannot fly.

WHAT ARE

The penguin is a flightless bird adapted to life in the sea.

Hummingbirds are so called because they flap their wings so fast they produce a hum.

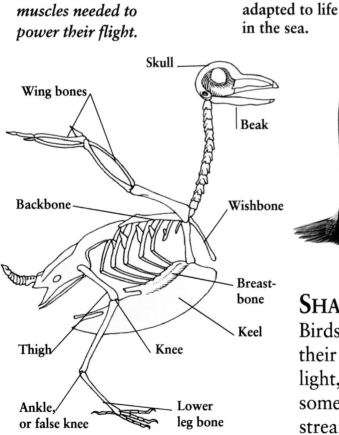

Skull

Wing bones

Beak

Backbone

Wishbone

Breast-bone

Keel

Thigh

Knee

Ankle, or false knee

Lower leg bone

SHAPES AND SIZES

Birds' wings, beaks and feet are adapted to their particular ways of life. Flying birds have light, streamlined bodies to aid flight. Even some flightless birds, such as penguins, are streamlined, for swimming underwater.

ON CLOSER INSPECTION
– *Hoatzin*

The hoatzin (right) of South America has very primitive characteristics. Nestlings are born with claws at their wing tips, much like those of *Archaeopteryx* (below). They use these along with their beaks and feet to climb about the trees.

BIRDS ?

The ostrich is a flightless bird that can run at a speed of 70 km/h.

The Andean condor is a huge bird with a 2.75-m wing span, which can soar at a height of 6,000 m.

Hummingbirds flap their wings so fast, they can hover before a flower to drink the nectar. Condors have broad wings for soaring aloft for long periods with little effort. Ostriches have given up the ability to fly and have developed powerful legs for running instead.

Bird evolution

During the time of the dinosaurs, the skies were ruled by bat-winged reptiles called pterosaurs. At this time, primitive birds, such as Archaeopteryx *(below) had developed feathers and were making a bid for the skies.* Archaeopteryx *is the earliest known bird. Although* Archaeopteryx *died out, other feathered relatives lived on to rule the skies when the pterosaurs disappeared.*

All birds and only birds have feather Feathers vary in size, shape and function. Wing feathers are essenti for flight. Tail feathers are needed for steering and stopping. Feathers also vary in colour. Some birds are mottled to blend in with their surroundings, while rainfore birds may be brightly coloured to hide among the bright flowers of the forest.

FEATHERS

Feather care
Birds take care of their feathers by preening. They draw their beaks through the feathers like a comb through hair. Birds also bathe their feathers in water and dust (above). Dust bathing scrubs dirt from the feathers.

Filoplumes (below) grow around flight and tail feathers, and sense the direction in which the feathers are lying.

This contour feather (left) gives the streamline shape to the bird's body.

These down feathers (left and above) keep the bird warm and are also used to line the nest.

This flight feather (above) of the outer wing helps give the bird power and lift in flight.

DIFFERENT TYPES OF FEATHERS
Feathers are made from a material called keratin, which is also used to make hair and fingernails. It is light, flexible and strong. There are four basic types of feather in a bird's plumage. The wing feathers lie together to make the perfect shape for flight. The tail feathers are essential

ON CLOSER INSPECTION
– Feathers and Humans

People have long used feathers for many decorative, ceremonial and practical purposes, such as for writing and as stuffing for pillows. North American tribes (right) fashioned head-dresses out of feathers to show great achievement.

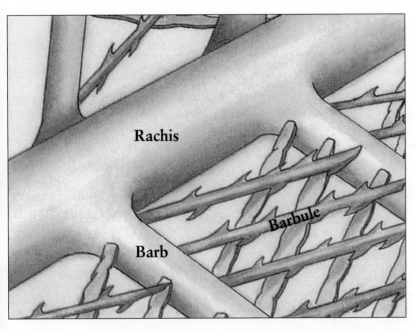

Feathers have a central quill, or rachis. Branching off from this are barbs. Barbs must form a continuous surface over which air can flow in flight. So they are locked together by tiny branches along their entire length called barbules (above). Barbules have tiny hooks on them that catch on the barbules of the next barb along. When barbules come undone birds preen them back together.

for steering in flight and they help a bird to balance when perched. They are often brightly coloured for use in courtship. Down feathers are fluffy and soft and trap a layer of air near a bird's skin to act as insulation. They provide more efficient insulation than fur. Contour feathers give the body a streamlined shape.

Camouflage

Plumage comes in many hues and patterns. Males are often more brightly coloured than females, in order to attract a mate. The mallard drake (male) displays his colourful plumage from the safety of the water. The duck (female) has drab colouring to blend in with her surroundings when she is sitting on her nest. This type of colouring is called camouflage and gives protection against predators.

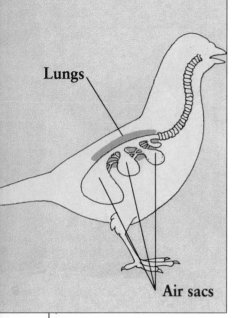

Lungs

Air sacs

Since the pterosaurs died out some 65 million years ago, birds have become the masters of the air. In flight, some birds can move faster than any other animal. They can travel farther than any land-living animal because mountains, lakes and seas are not necessarily barriers to them. They owe their success to the shape of their wings.

Fuelling flight

As a bird breathes in, air flows through the lungs into air sacs. As the bird breathes out, the air passes through the lungs again. Oxygen is absorbed both times. This supplies the great demand for energy during flight.

WINGS AND

WING SHAPE

The basic wing shape is that of an aerofoil, a shape which creates lift as air flows around it. The lift pulls the wing and the bird upwards when it flaps through the air and allows it to stay aloft when gliding.

The secondary flight feathers are shaped to help to provide lift.

The false wing, or alula, is a group of feathers that prevent stalling when a bird is flying slowly, such as when it is landing.

The large feathers of the outer wing are called the primary flight feathers. They produce the force for flight as the wing beats down.

ON CLOSER INSPECTION
– *Flight of the penguin*

Penguins (right) are flightless birds of the southern hemisphere. Their stiff wings have evolved into underwater flippers. These allow the bird to swim rapidly beneath the waves. They are covered with densely packed feathers for insulation.

FLIGHT

It is believed that no bird more than 22 kg in weight would be able to fly. The muscles of a bird over this weight would not be able to produce enough power to keep the bird aloft (see page 30).

THE ART OF FLAPPING

Birds beat their wings up and down for normal powered flight (right). As the wings beat downwards and forwards, they are spread wide. The primary flight feathers overlap to form a continuous surface. The downstroke produces high pressure under the wings, lifting the bird in the air.

On the upstroke, the bird curves its wings to make the surface smaller. It separates and twists its flight feathers. The air flows easily through them and they are easier for the bird to lift. The upstroke does not produce any lift.

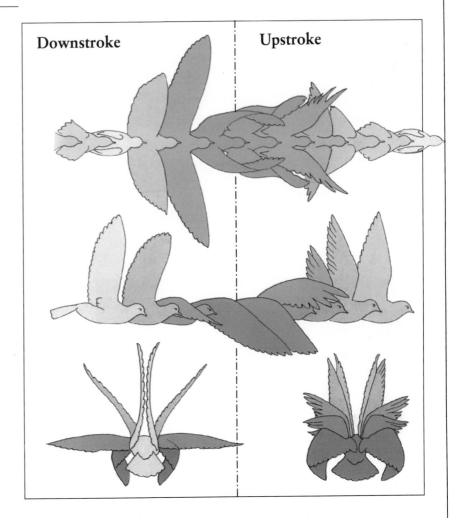

Downstroke   Upstroke

ings vary in shape according to the bird's way of life. The short rounded wings of finches allow them to twist and turn quickly in the air. The vulture has long, broad wings that allow it to stay aloft on rising hot currents of air. Swifts have long, curved wings for high-speed flight.

WAYS OF

Hovering

Hovering takes up a lot of energy. Kestrels (above) can hover for a short time over their prey just before swooping in for the kill. Hummingbirds hold their bodies at a 45-degree angle when hovering so that they beat their wings back and forth instead of up and down. This forces air downwards all the time.

LAUNCHING

To take off, most birds lean forwards, bend their legs, spread their wings and leap into the air with powerful down-strokes from their wings (below). Some larger birds, such as albatrosses, have more difficulty in taking off due to their great weight. They must run with their wings spread to give them the lift needed to launch themselves into the air.

LANDING

When coming in to land (below), a bird pulls its body upright, stretches its legs out forwards towards its perch, the ground or water. It spreads its tail wide to slow itself down. It beats its wings rapidly against the direction it is going. A part of the wing called the alula is raised to control air flow over the wing to prevent stalling in mid-air.

Alula

ON CLOSER INSPECTION
– Flight patterns

Birds can be recognised by the way they fly. Eagles have a soaring flight, circling high in the air. Chaffinches close their wings after quick bursts of flapping. They have an up-and-down flight pattern. Ducks flap continuously.

Eagle

Chaffinch

Mallard

FLYING

Albatross

SOARING ON HOT AIR

Land birds with broad, rounded wings, such as eagles (right), vultures and buzzards, can soar high in the sky, only occasionally needing to flap their wings. They achieve this by using the uplift produced from rising columns of hot air called thermals. The sun heats the ground, which, in turn, heats the air above it. Hot air is lighter than cold air and it begins to rise. Cold air sinks around the column and may undercut it. This produces a rising bubble of hot air in which the bird can circle. This type of flying is called thermal soaring.

Golden eagle

Soaring over the sea

Large sea birds have long, pointed wings and glide well. These birds include albatrosses (above), frigate birds, gulls, shearwaters and ospreys. The birds head into the wind over the sea. The air flowing over their wings creates lift. They rise higher and higher without flapping their wings to where the winds are stronger than they are at sea level. Then they turn and, gathering speed, they swoop downwards before turning again into the wind to rise again. This is called dynamic soaring.

The Egyptian vulture (below) is a scavenger, searching out the remains of food from other animals. Eggs form an important part of its diet. It picks up small eggs in its beak and then drops them onto rocks to smash them open. It then feeds on the runny insides. Larger eggs, like ostrich eggs, are too big to pick up. So the vultures pick up rocks and drop them on the eggs instead. Frigate birds are pirates more than scavengers. They harass other sea birds until they drop the food they are carrying. The frigate birds then swoop down and catch the food before it hits the water.

irds have to use their tough, lightweight beaks for catching and handling their food. Over time, birds' beaks have become the ideal shape to handle the food they eat, such as the long, slim beak of the curlew, used for probing in soft mud. A few birds, such as parrots and hawks, can also use their feet either to catch their food or to handle it.

BEAKS AND

Sunbirds feed on nectar. They have long, slim beaks

for probing into flowers to drink their sugary food.

The finch's short beak can exert the great force needed to crack seeds.

BEAK SHAPE

There seem to be as many ways of feeding as there are sources of food. Birds exploit an enormous range of food sources. Vultures have the hooked beak of meat-eaters. This shape is also found in birds of prey. The beak is used for tearing flesh into smaller swallowable pieces. Parrots have a hook for tearing into fruit instead of flesh, and the beak is short

ON CLOSER INSPECTION
– *Grub on a stick*

In the Galapagos Islands lives a bird, called the woodpecker finch, that actually uses a tool to help it hunt and catch its prey (right). It feeds on grubs and insects. As its name suggests, it finds these in holes in wood. Instead of digging them out with its beak, it spears them with a sharp twig or thorn held in its beak.

FEEDING

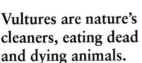

Vultures are nature's cleaners, eating dead and dying animals.

Blue jays are omnivores. Their beaks are not specialised in shape.

Flycatchers have bristles around their mouths to help catch insects.

Water feeders

Water feeders are no less varied in their feeding methods than other birds. Flamingos feed with their heads upside down and filter shrimps from the water. The skimmer swoops across the surface of the water with the lower half of its beak beneath the surface. As soon as it strikes a fish, it snaps it up immediately. The avocet has an up-curving beak and skims the surface slime for insects and grubs.

Flamingo

Skimmer

Avocet

and powerful enough to crack seeds. Birds that eat a wide range of foods, such as blue jays and blackbirds, have pointed beaks for picking up small seeds and insects. The extra length allows them to pick up larger grubs and worms. Flycatchers have broad, sharp beaks with which they peck up insects or catch them in mid-air. Geese have broad beaks to tear up the grass upon which they feed. They don't digest it very well and must eat almost constantly.

L

ike its beak, a bird's feet are adapted to its lifestyle and habitat. There are three basic types with many different variations. Perching feet have toes that can curl tightly round a branch. Feet for walking have long, straight toes. Feet for swimming are webbed or have flaps.

PADDLES ANI

Sturdy waddlers

Penguins are well adapted for life in the sea. On land their stubby legs seem clumsy and weak; but they are sturdy, and some penguins (above) can walk for miles from the sea to their breeding grounds.

Runners

The ostrich (below) is too heavy to fly. It has long, powerful legs with only two toes. These are specialised for running.

Eagles have three front toes for grasping prey. The back toe stabs the prey like a knife.

The two back toes allow the woodpecker to grip a tree trunk facing downwards.

FOOT SHAPES AND SIZES

Most birds have four toes instead of five like reptiles and mammals, but some only have three. Woodpeckers and other tree climbers have two in front and two behind for a firm grip. Eagles and hawks have feet designed for killing and carrying prey. They have sharp, curved talons. Their legs and feet are very strong, but because their curved

On Closer Inspection
– *Combing claws*

Some birds use their feet as well as their beaks for preening. Herons and bitterns (right) comb their feathers with tiny teeth on their claws. Nightjars have comb-like middle claws with which to clean moth scales off their feathers.

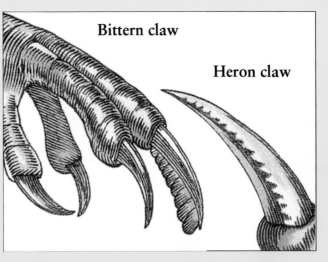

Bittern claw

Heron claw

CLAWS

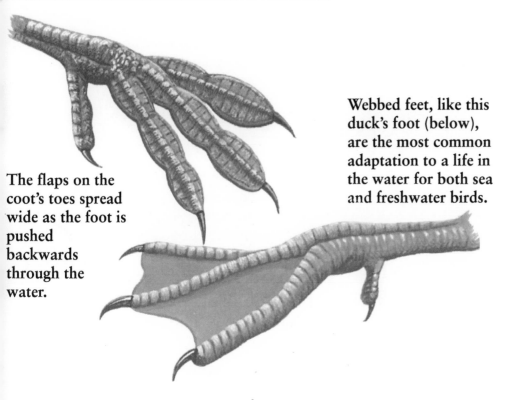

The flaps on the coot's toes spread wide as the foot is pushed backwards through the water.

Webbed feet, like this duck's foot (below), are the most common adaptation to a life in the water for both sea and freshwater birds.

Weak feet
Swifts and frigate birds are marvellous fliers, but their legs and feet are small and weak. The swift (above) cannot walk or hop along the ground; it can only perch in one place. The frigate bird lives by the sea, but the webbing on its feet is too small and its legs are too weak for it to swim well. Grebes are excellent paddlers, but reluctant fliers and weak walkers because their legs are too far back to balance well.

talons are so long, they have trouble walking. Mallards and other ducks, geese, swans and seabirds have webbed feet for paddling. They also act as brakes when the birds are landing on water. The coot, another water bird, has flaps on its feet. The flaps help it to swim and also prevent it from sinking into mud, like the duck's webbing.

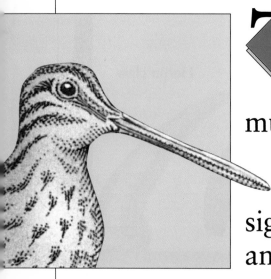

The senses of sight and hearing are the most important for the vast majority of birds. These senses are much more acute in birds than they are in humans. Birds have flatter eyeballs tha[n] humans. This means that everything [in] sight, both near and far, is in focus. Smell and taste are not so well developed in bird[s.]

Touch
In many long-beaked birds, such as snipes (above), the tip of the beak is rich in touch receptors. These birds hunt for food by probing with their sensitive beaks in mud.

Penguin sight
Penguins do not have binocular vision at all. When hunting for fish underwater, they use sound rather than sight, like dolphins, to locate their prey.

SENSES

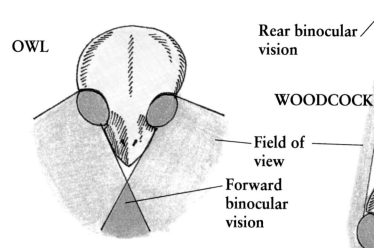

OWL

Rear binocular vision

WOODCOCK

Field of view

Forward binocular vision

FIELD OF VIEW
Owls have eyes on the front of the head. Both eyes see almost the same view. This is called binocular vision – binocular means "with two eyes". It allows animals to judge distances and is important to hunters. Woodcocks have eyes on both sides of the head. They have all-round vision with each eye seeing a different view. They can spot predators from any direction. Binocular vision is not so important to them.

Forward binocular vision

ON CLOSER INSPECTION
– Smelling for food

The kiwi (right) is a flightless bird of New Zealand. It has poor eyesight. It hunts for worms and grubs using its keen sense of smell. It has a long, slender beak with nostrils at the tip rather than at the base. It can smell food about 10 cm underground.

ECHO LOCATION

Oilbirds of South America and cave swiftlets of Asia nest in dark caves. Like bats, they have developed the ability to navigate using sound, called echo location. As they enter their caves, they produce clicks, which rebound off the cave walls. By listening to the echo, they know the position of the cave walls or their nest ledges. This ability is not as well developed as in bats.

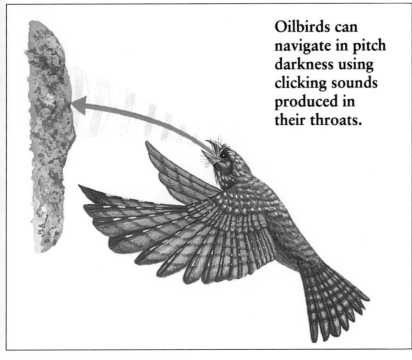

Oilbirds can navigate in pitch darkness using clicking sounds produced in their throats.

Owls

Owls have excellent sight, but even more excellent hearing. They do not have external ears. The ear-like feather tufts on this owl's head (above) have nothing to do with hearing. The ears of many owls are at different levels. Each ear receives sound at a slightly different time. This enables it to pinpoint prey in the dark without the aid of sight.

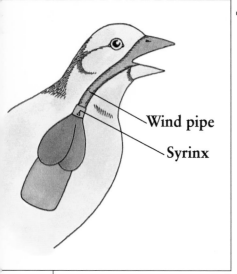

Wind pipe

Syrinx

early all birds have a voice. They either call or sing. A call is a single squawk or peep. A song is a series of notes following a fairly definite pattern. Half of all known birds both call and sing. Most waterbirds and birds of prey call but don't sing. Pelicans and some storks have no voice.

Syrinx

Birds have a voice box, or syrinx (above), at the bottom of the wind pipe (instead of high in the throat as in humans). Tiny muscles in the voice box control all the sounds that birds can make. They cannot alter the sounds with their tongues and have no teeth or lips. Therefore birds can sing with their beaks open or closed.

Other forms of communication

Some birds produce sounds other than with their voices to communicate. Male grouse (below) beat their wings to produce a drumming noise in the breeding season. Woodpeckers drum on tree trunks with their beaks not just for food but also to advertise their presence to others.

COMMUN

SONGBIRDS

It is usually only the male birds who sing chiefly in the mating season. They sing from various perches around their territories. This is called an "advertising song". It warns other males to stay away and it attracts a mate.

ON CLOSER INSPECTION
– Talented mimics

Some birds mimic songs of other birds and also the sounds around them. Starlings are very skillful mimics. Parrots (right) and minas become mimics only in captivity. They are often trained to mimic human speech and whistling.

CATION

Bullfinches have a soft, piping song.

CHICKS

Chicks have at least two calls. One type of call tells the parent birds that the chicks are hungry (below). Another call tells the parents that they are either frightened or hurt.

These bullfinch chicks are calling to their parent for food.

Adult birds

In woodlands where the trees stop animals from seeing very far, birds communicate almost entirely by sound. Finches have as many as 25 different calls. Some of them are also understood by other kinds of birds. They have different calls to indicate a threat from the sky or from the ground.

Impressive pouch

The male frigate bird has a red throat pouch. He inflates it with air during the mating season until it looks like a big red balloon under his beak (below). With this display he hopes to attract females. But the male frigate may have to sit there inflated for several hours until a female shows interest in him and comes over to join him.

Courtship is often the most spectacular form of bird communication. It is usually up to the male (cock) to attract the female (hen). This leads to fierce competition between males. Ways of wooing the female include displaying plumage, showing off singing, dancing, feeding or nest-building skills. Successful males pass on characteristics to the next generation through mating.

COURTSHIP

Building

The male bower bird (below) builds a kind of shelter on the ground with twigs. Then he decorates it with all sorts of colourful items to attract a mate.

PAIRING UP

Courtship creates a bond between mates. Some birds bond for one season only and part company as soon as the chicks are grown. Some, such as swans, ducks, geese and storks, bond for life. The hen harrier bonds with several females who build their nests in his territory.

Singing

The thrush (left) is a songbird. During the courting season, the male sings his advertising song from different perches in his territory so other males will move on but females may stop.

On Closer Inspection
– *Blue birds of paradise*

Male birds of paradise are among the most strikingly beautiful birds in the world. They grow plumage of spectacular colours, which they display to attract females, sometimes in the most remarkable fashion. The blue bird of paradise (right) displays by hanging upside down in a tree and spreading his electric blue plumage while producing a noise like a siren.

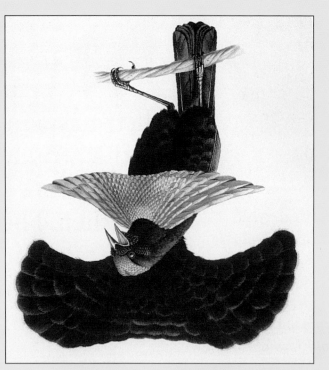

AND DISPLAY

Feeding
Male roseate terns present their mate with food (left). This shows the female that the male will be a good provider because she will need more food when producing eggs.

Display
During the courting season, male ruffs (right) meet to display in a set area called a "lek". They expand feathers around their throats and pose. The females mate with the most dominant male.

Dance
Cranes (above) have an elaborate courtship display. The male bows to the female, then jumps up and down, trumpeting until she responds. She performs movements resembling his and they appear to dance together.

Oven bird
Rufous ovenbirds (above) of South America build great balls of clay to nest in, which look like old-fashioned ovens.

Puffins
Puffins (below) nest by the sea in colonies. They lay their eggs either in old burrows left by other animals, or in burrows which they dig themselves.

ot all birds build nests. Nightjars and some falcons lay their eggs on bare ground. Some birds build their nests in tree hollows or in burrows in the ground. Many species make their nests secure by cementing the materials together. Thrushes and blue jays use mud. Hummingbirds use spider webs. Swifts use their own gummy saliva, which also cements the nest in place.

CUP NEST
The cup nest, like that of the goldcrest (below), is the most familiar nest shape. Each type of bird has its own variation of shape and materials, and the builder of a nest can be identified from the nest's shape and materials used. The goldcrest builds its nest from moss and cobwebs in the outer branches of trees away from predators. The chaffinch also uses spider web. The nest is then constructed with moss and grass and lined with down.

NEST-

On Closer Inspection – Communal living

Weavers are small birds that live in Africa and Asia. They often build nests in large numbers in the same tree. The sociable weavers (right) of South Africa build a communal roof in a tree. Then each pair of birds builds a nest underneath it like a hanging basket. The nests are intricately woven from grasses and reeds.

BUILDING

SPIT AND MUD

Swallows (right) build nests against walls or cliffs, in caves or under the roofs of buildings. They build the cup-shaped nest with mud pellets, reinforced with grass. They fly in search of puddles with just the right kind of mud. Swallows often nest quite close together. They feed on the wing so do not compete for ground-based territories.

Tailoring

Tailorbirds (below) live in Asia and Australia. They are remarkable because they sew or rivet living leaves together to form a pouch for their nest. They use their beaks as a needle and plant fibres as thread.

Egg variety

Eggs laid out in the open are usually coloured to blend in with their surroundings, such as plover eggs (below). Owl eggs are hidden from view – they need no colouring to hide them (below). Guillemots lay their eggs on bare rock ledges by the sea. They are pointed at one end (below). This makes them swivel around in a circle instead of rolling off a cliff edge.

As soon as the nest is completed, egg laying begins. Many species produce an egg a day, but larger birds take longer to form eggs. The size o the clutch (the number of eggs) depends on a bird's survival chances. The albatros has good chances of survival and a long life, so it produces only one egg. The duck usually has many predators. It lays up to 20 eggs to make sure some survive.

EGGS AND

An owl's plain white egg

A guillemot's pointed egg

Camouflaged plover's eggs

EGG DEVELOPMENT

Inside a newly laid egg, the undeveloped chick, or embryo (1), is on the surface of the yolk (2). The yolk and egg white, or albumen (3), provide all the food for the embryo as it develops. An egg tooth grows on the chick's beak just before it is ready to hatch (4). The egg tooth helps the chick to break the shell apart (5). The amount of time it takes for the chick to develop inside the egg varies depending on the type of bird.

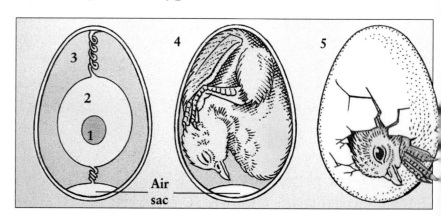

ON CLOSER INSPECTION
– Mallee Fowl

The male mallee fowl of Australia (right) builds a huge mound of vegetation covered with sand. The female lays her eggs in it. The eggs are incubated by the heat of the rotting vegetation. The male maintains the temperature of the nest mound. The chicks dig their way out about four months later.

HATCHING

Two types of chick

Newly hatched chicks need differing amounts of care. Birds such as plovers (above), ducks and pheasants hatch out ready to leave the nest. They can see, walk and feed themselves. Other birds including finches and falcons are born naked and blind (below). They depend on their parents for food. They remain in the nest until they can fly away.

HATCHING

When a bird is ready to hatch, it first breaks a small hole in the egg so that it can start to breathe properly. This is exhausting work and the chick may then rest for several hours or even days. Once rested the final stage of hatching usually takes less than an hour.

Twice a year many birds make a great journey. This is called migration. During the northern summer, they breed in northern lands, suc as Europe and North America. Here there is plenty of space and food. Before winter sets in, they and their offspring migrate south in search of food and warmer weather. In spring, they set off north again

V-formation
Many waterfowl such as geese, swans and ducks, migrate in a v-formation (above). They take it in turns to lead the flock. The lead bird creates a flow of air which pulls on the birds behind, helping them fly.

ROUTES
The map (right) shows the routes of some north-south migrators. Some Arctic terns travel a record 36,000 km from pole to pole and back. The journey of the skua is almost as long. The common swift and willow warbler breed in Europe and Russia

MIGRATION

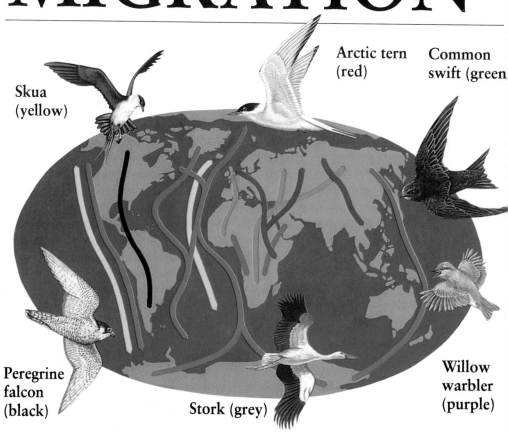

Skua (yellow)

Arctic tern (red)

Common swift (green

Peregrine falcon (black)

Stork (grey)

Willow warbler (purple)

and overwinter in Africa and southeast Asia. The stork crosses the equator, travelling between northern Africa and southern Africa. American peregrine falcons travel from northern Canada to the southern end of South America.

ON CLOSER INSPECTION
– *Hibernation*

In the Colorado Desert of North America lives the poorwill (right), the only bird that hibernates. In winter, as food becomes scarce, these birds hibernate in rock crevasses. Their breathing and heart rate slow down and their body temperature drops by half.

MIGRATION IN FLOCKS

Many birds migrate in huge flocks. A flock of starlings (below) can have up to a million birds. Travelling in flocks allows parents to guide their offspring to warmer lands. It also gives individual birds more protection from predators – safety in numbers.

NAVIGATION TECHNIQUES

Travelling by day, birds navigate using landmarks, such as rivers and valleys, and the position of the sun. Some birds migrate at night. They are partly guided by the stars. Some birds, like pigeons, seem to be sensitive to the Earth's magnetic field and use this to navigate.

Swans are among the heaviest flying birds.

AMAZING BIRD FACTS

High fliers Bar-headed geese (below) are among the highest fliers. They migrate over the Himalayas in Asia. Bar-headed geese have been detected at more than 7,500 metres high.

Sky diving Peregrine falcons are the fastest living creatures. When stooping from a great height, they partly fold in their wings to improve streamlining and dive at speeds of more than 300 km/h.

Size of a bee The smallest bird in the world is the bee hummingbird. It grows to 57 mm in length. Half of this is taken up by the tail and beak. Hummingbirds also build the smallest nests. That of the bee hummingbird is the size of a thimble.

No other bird can match the peregrine falcon for speed when it is diving on a kill.

Deep-sea diving The penguin is the most adapted bird to a life at sea. Emperor penguins are the largest penguins and the deepest divers. Using their wings to propel themselves, emperor penguins have been detected at depths of 250 m.

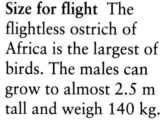

Size for flight The flightless ostrich of Africa is the largest of birds. The males can grow to almost 2.5 m tall and weigh 140 kg.

Marathon migrator The Arctic tern travels farther in one year than any other bird. It breeds in the Arctic in the summer. It then flies the 18,000 km to the Antarctic to escape the Arctic winter. When summer comes back, the bird returns to breed.

Wild population The most numerous bird in the wild is the African red-billed quelea, a seed-eating weaver bird. It has an adult population of about 1,500 million.

Heavy-weight fliers The heaviest individual flying bird ever recorded was a mute swan that weighed 22.5 kg. The heaviest species of flying bird is the African Kori bustard, which reaches 19 kg in weight.

Aerofoil A shape, with a curved top surface and a flatter lower surface, like the wing of a bird or an aircraft. As air flows over it, the wing is lifted upwards.

Alula Also called the false wing, it is held open when a bird slows down to land. It prevents the bird from stalling and falling.

Archaeopteryx This was the first known bird and lived over 150 million years ago. It was the size of a gull, had sharp teeth like a lizard and was a poor flier.

Barb These grow out from either side of the rachis of a feather.

Barbule These extend from either side of the barbs of a feather. They have tiny hooks along their lengths and lock the barbs together.

Binocular vision Each eye has a slightly different field of view. You have binocular vision where the two fields overlap. This is important for judging distances.

Carnivore An animal that feeds on the flesh of other animals.

Embryo A developing baby animal before it is born or hatches.

Habitat The natural home of an animal.

Hibernate To sleep throughout the cold winter months.

Insulation A covering to stop heat escaping.

Omnivore An animal that eats both plants and the flesh from other animals.

Overwinter To spend the winter in a place. Many birds overwinter in warmer places.

Pectoral muscles The large chest muscles in a bird used in flight.

Plumage A collective name for a bird's feathers.

Preening Using the beak to clean feathers and to repair damaged feathers by hooking the barbs together again.

GLOSSARY

Pterosaurs Flying reptiles with bat-like wings that died out 65 million years ago.

Rachis The hollow central shaft of a feather, also called the quill.

Scavenger An animal that feeds on the left-overs of food from other animals.

Stalling Slowing down in flight and stopping in mid-air.

Stoop To swoop or dive out of the sky.

Streamline A special shape that allows air or water to pass around it with little resistance.

Thermal A rising column of hot air.

Vertebrate An animal with a backbone.

Warm-blooded An animal that can keep its body at a constant temperature.

INDEX

Photo credits

Abbreviations: t-top, m-middle, b-bottom, r-right, l-left

Title page, 2-3, 5, 23, 27b, 28, 29: Frank Spooner Pictures; 7, 8, 12, 16, 18, 20, 25, 27t, 30: Bruce Coleman Collection.